STITCH BY STITCH

by the same author

MISS PATCH'S LEARN-TO-SEW BOOK

STITCH BY STITCH

NEEDLEWORK FOR BEGINNERS

Written and illustrated by

Carolyn Meyer

HARCOURT BRACE JOVANOVICH, INC.

NEW YORK

CDEFGHIJ

Hardbound edition ISBN 0-15-280350-5
Library edition ISBN 0-15-280351-3

Library of Congress Catalog Card Number: 77-117618

PRINTED IN THE UNITED STATES OF AMERICA

For my mother

Contents

STITCH BY STITCH

Introduction

Needles have been used to make beautiful things for thousands of years. People have stitched delicate embroidery on their clothes and created enormous tapestries for their walls. They have made simple cotton coverlets for their beds and sewed elegant linen cloths for their tables.

Not long ago every girl began when she was very young—sometimes only five or six years old—to fill a hope chest with practical things that she had made and decorated herself. By the time she was ready to marry, the chest was ready with the things she would need for her home.

Young girls today don't have to fill a hope chest with their needlework before they marry. So there are really only two reasons for you to learn to do needlework at all: to make beautiful things and to have fun doing it.

CHAPTER 1

Beginning

Embroidery is really very much like ordinary sewing.
(In the beginning it is ordinary;
later on it can become quite *extra*ordinary!)

If you know how to make a *running stitch*,
you already know one of the first embroidery stitches.

If you have a piece of striped cloth
or one with a large, simple pattern on it,
you can practice the stitch you know and learn some new ones
while you are actually making something:

a needlework bag   a place mat

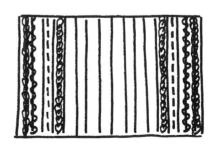

What You'll Need

CLOTH: Any odd pieces you have are good for learning to make the stitches, but plain cotton makes learning easier. As you get to know more stitches, you will want to try using different kinds of cloth, such as linen and wool. Therefore, begin now to save pretty pieces to work on later.

YARN: 6-strand embroidery floss
or crewel yarn
or other wool or synthetic yarn
(orlon, nylon, acrilan)

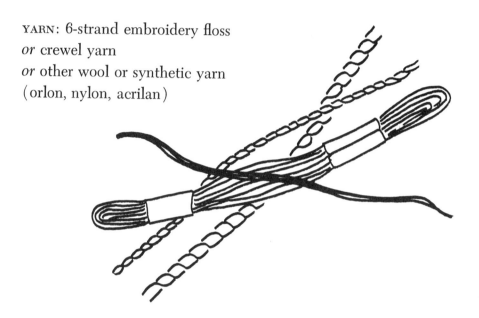

Use colors that match or mix well with the cloth. Use heavy yarn on heavy cloth and light-weight yarn on thin cloth. If you are making something that is to be washed, remember that wool must be washed *very* carefully by hand, and you might rather use something else.

NEEDLE: With an eye just large enough for the yarn to go through.

12

EMBROIDERY HOOP: To keep the cloth flat while you are working. If you don't have a hoop, you will have to be very careful not to pull the thread too tight or your work will be puckered.

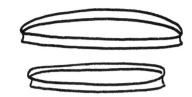

SCISSORS: Small ones for clipping yarn and thread, larger ones for cutting out cloth.

THIMBLE: You'll get a sore finger if you don't use one.

DRAWING TOOLS (for drawing designs right on the cloth): Washable colored pencils, or washable fine-tipped markers, or dressmakers' chalk, or an ordinary pencil.

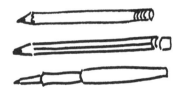

NEEDLEWORK BAG: Directions on page 20 for making your own. In the meantime, any box or bag will do.

SHOES

SUPER MARKET

Getting Started

Try out your stitches on a scrap of cloth, but first...

Put the cloth in the hoop.
Separate the two rings of the hoop and spread the cloth
over the smaller ring. Push the larger ring down over it.
Gently pull the cloth on the outside of the hoop to take out
any wrinkles and make it tight.

Hold the hoop in your left hand
with your thumb on top.
You will be using that thumb often
to hold down the thread
while the right hand makes the stitch
(if you are right-handed).

Your thumb should reach easily to the place where you will be
stitching. If your thumb must stretch too far, take off the hoop
and move the part where you are working closer to the hoop.

Thread the needle.
If you are using embroidery floss, cut off a piece as long as
your arm. Usually you will want to work with three strands.
Wrap the other three around an empty matchbook or a spool
to use later.

Use the three strands as though they
were one. They will go through
the eye of the needle more easily
if you wet them a little
on the tip of your tongue
and then twist the ends together.
Leave one end long and one short.

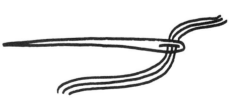

If you are using yarn, you can try
to thread the needle the same way.
But if the yarn frays, try it this way:

Make a tiny loop of the yarn
with the needle inside the loop.

Squeeze the loop with your thumb
and finger to make it as small
as possible, and slide out the needle.

Then try to push that loop
through the eye.
Leave one end long and one short.

Make a knot in the long end.
Wet your finger a little on the tip
of your tongue, and wrap the yarn
around your finger once.

Roll it off your thumb
and pull it tight.
The knot should be small and neat,
but don't worry if it's not
because it will be hidden
on the wrong side.

15

Beginning Stitches

The size of the stitch depends partly on the yarn
(bigger stitches for heavier yarn)
and partly on the design you want to make.
Usually you will want to keep
stitches of one kind all the same size.

RUNNING STITCHES:
Work from right ← to left.
Come up with the needle
from the wrong side.
Make several stitches that are
the same size on the right side
of the cloth as on the wrong side.

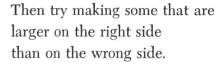

Then try making some that are
larger on the right side
than on the wrong side.

And the other way around.

Sometimes you can combine two sizes.

BACK STITCHES:
Make a row of dots with colored pencil or marker
a little less than one-quarter of an inch apart,
like this . . . . . to show you where to make
the stitches. Work from right ← to left.
Come up with the needle
from the wrong side
at the first dot
and go down at the second dot.

Come up at the third dot
and go down again at the second dot.

Come up at the fourth dot
and go down at the third.
Always count two dots to the left to come up
and one dot to the right to go down.

When you can do this, try making the stitches without the dots.

OUTLINE STITCHES:
Make a row of dots to show you where to make the stitches.
Work from left → to right.
Come up with the needle
from the wrong side
at the first dot and
go down at the third dot.

Come up again at the second dot
and go down at the fourth dot.
Always count two dots to the right to go down
and one dot to the left to come up.
As you go along, be sure your thread always
hangs down below the row of stitches. If it is
sometimes above and sometimes below,
the stitches will not be the same.

Now try making the stitches without the dots.

SPLIT STITCHES:

Work from left → to right.
This stitch works better with yarn
than with embroidery thread.
Come up from the wrong side.
Work it like the *outline stitch*,
but make each stitch in two steps:
First go down and pull the yarn through.
Then come up right through
the middle of the stitch
and "split" the yarn.

CHAIN STITCHES:

Make a row of dots to show you
where to make the stitches.
Work from right ← to left.
Come up with the needle
from the wrong side
at the first dot.
Hold the thread against the cloth
with your left thumb
and go down again
right next to the same dot.

Come up at the second dot
and pull the thread through.
The loop that forms will get smaller
as you pull the thread tight.
Don't pull it *too* tight.

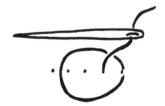

Hold down the thread again.
Go down right next to the second dot,
inside the finished loop,
and come up at the third dot.

Pull the thread through.

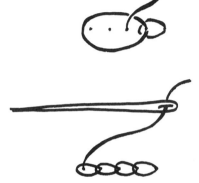

Each stitch is a link that holds the one before it in place.
Now try making the stitches without the dots.

Fastening Off

When you come to the end of each row or group of stitches, or when you are changing threads, push the needle through to the wrong side, turn your work over, and weave the needle in and out of the backs of several stitches. Be careful not to sew through the cloth when you are fastening off.

Making a Needlework Bag

You will need two square pieces of cloth about 15 inches wide and 15 inches long to make a handy bag for your needlework. You can make it smaller or larger if you want to.

Choose cloth that is strong, but not so heavy that you will have a hard time sewing on it. Look for a simple design of plants or animals. If you can't find anything that you like, make up your own design or copy a pattern from a book or magazine onto plain cloth with colored pencils or markers. Keep the design near the center of the squares.

Study the design and decide how you are going to use the stitches that you know. You can do all the stitches in yarn of one color, or you can pick a different color for each part of the design. You can also use a different color for each kind of stitch.

BACK STITCH AND OUTLINE STITCH

Sometimes you can make two rows of stitches next to each other —the same kind or different— when you want to make one line show up more. And you can fill in a whole area by working several rows right next to each other.

CHAIN STITCH AND SPLIT STITCH

SWIMMING FISH, RUNNING STITCH

Put the cloth in the embroidery hoop and stitch the design.
You do not need to go over every line—just the ones you want to
bring out. Make most of your stitches in the part of the design
that is in the center of the square of cloth. Finish stitching
the design on both squares before you begin to sew up the bag.

Put the two squares together
with the right sides on the inside.
Pin the two side edges. Measure
and mark half an inch from each side
for seams. Baste the seams
with large *running stitches*.
Sew the seams with small *running stitches*.
Every four or five stitches,
make a *back stitch* to make the
seam stronger. At the end
of each seam, fasten off the thread
by making three extra little stitches
right on top of each other.

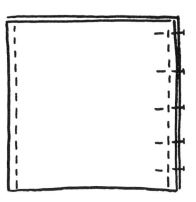

Measure and mark one inch from the top
for a hem. Fold down the hem
toward the wrong side and press it
with your fingers or a warm iron.
Turn under a little bit of the
cut edge and pin it all around.

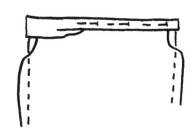

Baste it with large *running stitches*.
Sew it with little *hemming stitches*.

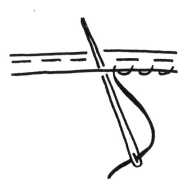

21

With the bag still wrong side out,
measure and mark three inches from each
side seam. Fold the two sides of the
bag along the marks, bringing the
side seams toward the center.
Pin it across the bottom.
Measure and mark half an inch
from the bottom for a seam.
Baste the seam with large
running stitches. Then sew it
with small *running stitches*
and some *back stitches*.
When you turn the bag right side out,
there will be a pleat on each side,
like a shopping bag.
Press the pleat carefully to give
the bag a squared-off shape.

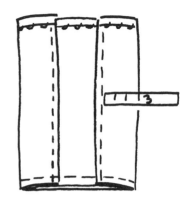

To make the handles, cut two strips
of cloth 15 inches long and
4 inches wide. Fold each strip
in half the long way and crease it
with your fingers.
Then fold the edges in to meet
at the crease. Fold it up again
and pin the opening. Baste it
with large *running stitches*
and sew it along the open edge
with small *running stitches*.
Sew a handle on each side of the bag.
Sew it inside near the pleat
with *hemming stitches*.
Go over the stitches two more times.

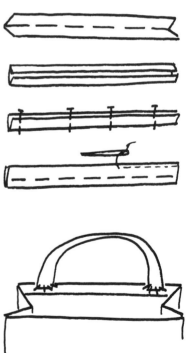

Dressing Up the Stitches

You will discover more ways to use beginning stitches when you have learned ways to dress them up a bit. By weaving thread back and forth through them, you can make these plain stitches look very fancy.

THREADED STITCHES: Work a row of *running stitches* that are long on the right side of the cloth and short on the wrong side. Then, with thread of a different color, come up from the wrong side at the beginning of the row. Weave the needle back and forth through the stitches. Don't go through the cloth. Pull the thread tight, or leave it loose to make little loops.

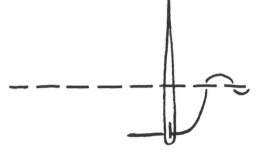

When you come to the end of the row, turn your work and weave back in the other direction.

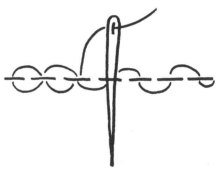

Next, try weaving back and forth through a row of *back stitches.*

WHIPPED STITCHES: Work a row of *running stitches* that are long on the right side of the cloth and short on the wrong side. Then, with thread of a different color, come up from the wrong side at the beginning of the row. Slide the needle through each stitch, always going through from above the row of stitches. This wraps the thread around the *running stitches.*

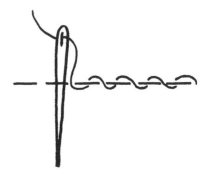

Next, try wrapping—
or *whipping,* as it is called
—a row of *back stitches.*

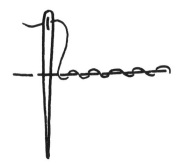

CHINESE (PEKINGESE) STITCH: Work a row of *back stitches.*
Then, with thread of a different
color, come up from the wrong side
at the end of the row.
Slide the needle *up* through
the second *back stitch.*
(Be careful not to go through
the cloth, but between the
cloth and the thread.)
Slide it *down* through the first stitch
and *up* again through the third stitch.
It will be prettier if you leave
the thread rather loose instead
of pulling it tight.

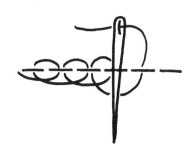

Making a Place Mat

You can use some of the stitches you know to decorate
a place mat. Striped cloth like ticking is very
good for this. But you can also use plain cloth and draw
a few lines on it to follow for making the stitches.

To make a place mat that is 16 inches long and 12 inches wide
when it is finished, you will need a piece of cloth
18 inches long and 14 inches wide, with the stripes going
from top to bottom. (The extra inches are for a hem on each edge.)

Use a ruler to measure. Use a colored pencil or marker to show you where to cut. Then measure one inch from each edge and draw a few very light lines to show you where the hems will be.

Choose yarn or thread in colors that will show up against the stripes. If you have black and white stripes, for instance, you could use red and pink thread. If the stripes are green and white, you could use orange and yellow thread.

Make several rows of stitches from the top hemline to the bottom hemline to form a band of stitches. Make a band about three inches wide on each end of the mat. Work the rows of stitches over the stripes or in between. Space the rows evenly, or make some rows close together and others far apart.

Use any combination of stitches you want, but use only one kind of stitch in each row. The bands of stitches should be similar, but they do not need to match.

You could start each band with a row of *running stitches*. Then a row of *threaded back stitches*. Next a row of *chain stitches*. Next a row of *whipped running stitches*. Next a row of *Chinese stitches*. Then work the pattern backward, ending with *running stitches*.

This is only a suggestion, and you should experiment to find what you like best.

After you have finished the bands of stitches,
you are ready to hem the place mat.

On the wrong side of the place mat,
measure half an inch from each edge and
make marks with colored pencil or
marker to show you where to fold the hem.
First fold the hem along one of the
long edges and crease it with
your fingers or a warm iron.
Then turn it over again
to make a double hem.

Pin the hem and baste it with
long *running stitches.* Sew it
with little *hemming stitches.*
Make the stitches very small,
picking up only one or two threads
on the right side, so that they
hardly show.
Hem the other long edge
and the two short edges.

You can also make a matching napkin.
Cut a 16-inch square of cloth.
Embroider a wide band down one side of
the napkin. You can use a pattern of
stitches like the one you made on the
place mat. Embroider a narrow band down
the other side. Use just part of the pattern
for the wide band. Hem it as you did
the place mat.

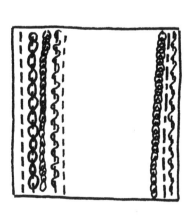

CHAPTER 2

Cross Stitches

The *cross stitch* is a very old and often used stitch.
Long ago it was done by counting threads in the cloth.
Sometimes the threads were so fine
that a girl who was careful could make a row
of twenty-two tiny crosses to an inch.
She could make animals and flowers and spell out
whole poems and prayers with tiny stitches.

A faster and easier way to learn this stitch is to work the crosses
on checked cloth. Gingham is woven with checks in several sizes,
but ¼-inch squares are the most common and are a good size to work
on. There are only four crosses to an inch, instead of twenty-two.

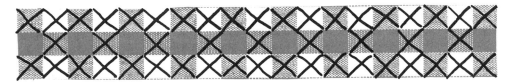

You can make *cross stitches* one at a time or in rows, depending
on how you are using them. It doesn't matter much which way
you work them, but it is important that the stitches always cross
in the same direction.

To make a single cross,
come up from the wrong side
at corner #1.
Cross over to corner #2.
Come up again at corner #3,
and cross over to corner #4.

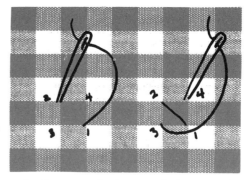

You can make the next *cross stitch* above or below or left or right
of the first one, but always cross the thread over in the same
order so that the stitches will all look the same.

To make a row of *cross stitches,*
work from right ← to left.
Come up from the wrong side
at corner #1.
Make all the stitches
from corner #1 to corner #2
to the end of the row.
Then work from left → to right
and make all the stitches
from corner #3 to corner #4
back to the beginning of the row
to finish the crosses.
Work the next row above or below.

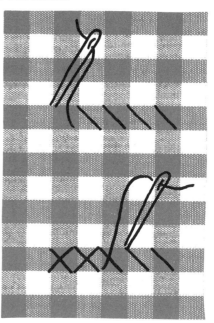

Next you will want to experiment with ways to use *cross stitches.*
They can be used to make simple borders.

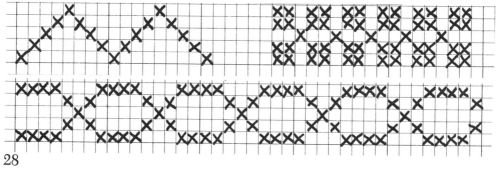

But they can also be used to make complicated-looking designs like these star and flower patterns and the heart and tulip. They are all very old designs.

They are really easy to do once you know exactly which squares you will be *cross-stitching*. Use a colored pencil or marker to put a dot in the center of each square that is to have a stitch in it.

It is usually easier to start at the center of the design and count out from there. Lay a ruler or piece of paper on the book as a guide. (The designs are shown much smaller here than they will appear on your work.)

Making a Potholder

Either the flower or the star design is a good choice for decorating a potholder. You will need two pieces of checked cloth, each 33 squares wide and 33 squares long. (That is 8¼ inches, but count to make sure the number of checks works out as it should.)

Draw around the pieces, but don't cut them out until you have finished stitching them. It is easier to fit a whole piece of cloth into your embroidery hoop rather than small pieces.

You will also need two squares cut from an old towel, or several squares cut from old sheets or other cloth, to make padding for the potholder.

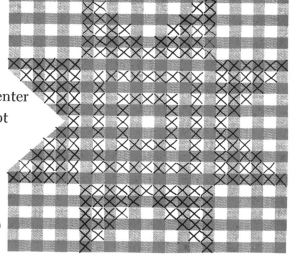

To find the center square, count in 17 from each side and mark it with a pin. Then count out from the center and mark with a colored dot each square that will have a *cross stitch* in it.

Choose embroidery floss in a color that will show up against both the colored and the white checks.

Stitch the design with three strands of floss. It is usually easier to start working from the upper-right corner, one stitch at a time, or in rows when you can.

Stitch the same or another design on the second piece of cloth, or leave it plain. Then cut out the squares, if you have not already done that.

Put the padding pieces cut
from towels or other cloth
on the wrong side of
both pieces of checked cloth
so that two rows of checks show
all around. Pin and baste them.
Turn them over to the right side.

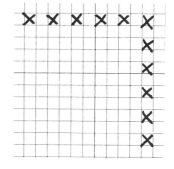

Count four rows from the edge
and make a border of *cross stitches*
all around, skipping every
other check and going
right through all the layers.
It would be clumsy to put
all of this into a hoop,
so keep your work flat and
don't pull the stitches too tight.
Do the same thing with the second piece.

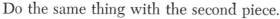

Put the two pieces together
with the right sides on the inside
and the padding on the outside.
Pin and baste them.

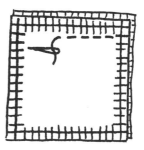

Sew around three sides
with little *running stitches*
along the second row of checks.
Turn your work right side out.

Turn to the inside
the two edges that are not sewed
and pin them together.
Sew them with little *overcast stitches*.

If you want to hang up your potholder, sew a loop of ribbon
or a metal ring in one corner.

Making a "Show Towel"

More than a hundred years ago, Pennsylvania German girls
learned to stitch fancy "show towels"
that were not meant to be used. They were only for decoration.
The one you make with their favorite heart and tulip pattern
and your initials (or the initials of the person
for whom you are making a gift) can be a *useful* decoration.

You will need a piece of checked cloth 100 squares long and
61 squares wide—that is, 25 inches by 15½ inches. Count up
14 squares from the bottom and count in 31 squares from the side
to find the starting place at the bottom of the heart.

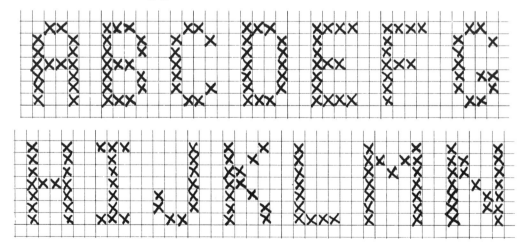

Then count and mark with
a colored dot each square
that will have a *cross stitch* in it.
Put an initial on each side
of the tulip stem.

You can use floss in different
colors for this design—
one color for the heart,
another for the tulip,
and a third color for the stem
and initials. Start working
the stitches from the bottom.

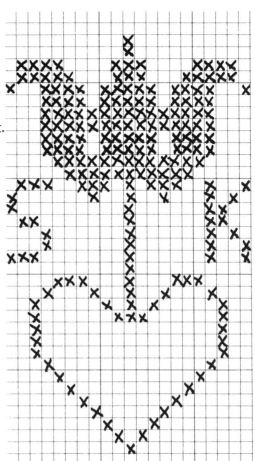

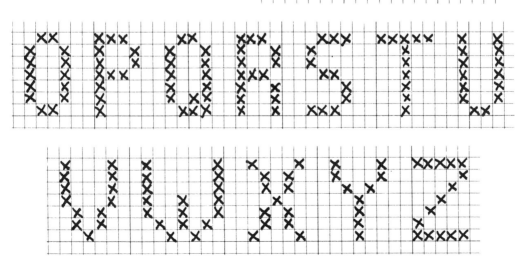

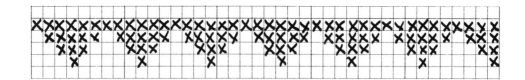

Make a border about an inch
wide (four squares)
below the design and
another across the top.
(Leave plain an inch
at each end of the towel for a hem.)
Use one of these borders
or invent one of your own.

Turn one row of checks
toward the wrong side
along the two long edges of the towel.
Turn it over again
to make a double hem.
Press it with your fingers
or with a warm iron.
Pin it and baste it.
Sew it with little *hemming stitches*.

Make a double hem on the
top and bottom that is
two rows wide.

CHAPTER 3

More Stitches

There are stitches that are worked in even rows,
and there are stitches that are worked in even squares.
You know how to do both kinds.
But there are many more stitches
that can be worked any way you want to work them,
for making whatever you want to make.

Lazy Daisies

The *lazy daisy stitch* is one of the prettiest and most fun to do.
It is a little like the *chain stitch*, but the "links" are made separately,
and each stitch forms the petal of a flower or a leaf or even part of a
snowflake!

Use a coin or a button for a pattern
to draw a small circle on the cloth.
Come up from the wrong side
in the center of the circle.
Hold the thread against the
cloth with your left thumb.
Go down at almost the same spot
where you first came up.
Come up again on the edge
of the circle and
pull the thread through.
The loop that forms will get smaller
as you pull the thread tight.
Don't pull it too tight.

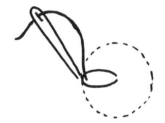

Now go down *outside* the loop,
but close to the place
where you came up.
This makes a tiny stitch
to hold down the end of the petal.

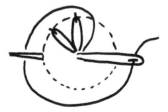

Come up again
near the center of the circle.
Make another petal the same way.
Turn your work as you go.

Experiment with ways to work
the *lazy daisy stitch.*
Work five or six petals
of the same size
that meet in the center
or leave an open center.

Try working them "freehand," without drawing a circle first.
The daisies will look different made with different kinds of thread.
Daisies worked with yarn look fuzzier than daisies worked in floss.

Work many long petals close
together, or petals of
different lengths.

Make a *long-tailed daisy*
with a small loop
and a big holding-down stitch.
Start on the outside of the circle
and make the holding-down stitch
toward the center of the flower.

Make a *double daisy* by first
working long petals around
an open center, and then
working short petals with
a closed center on top of it.
Try using thread in two colors
or shades of the same color.

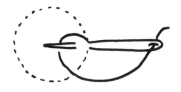

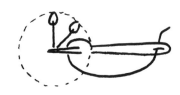

Try making the loops and
holding-down stitches
in different lengths.

You can also use single *lazy daisy stitches*
to make small leaves.
First make a "stem" with *outline stitches*.
Then add a few *lazy daisy stitches* at an angle
on each side of the stem.

Making a Notebook Cover

Lazy daisies will grow almost anywhere, but a good place to plant
your first ones is on the cover of a notebook, a matchbox, or
any other small object on which you can glue something.

Find a piece of cloth heavy enough so that the glue will not come through it. Decide what kind and colors of thread to use. Measure a small spiral-bound notebook. Draw its outline on the cloth.

Use coins or buttons to decide where to put the flowers. You can line them up evenly or scatter them or bunch them. You can make them all the same size or different sizes. Make the design suit the shape of the notebook.

When you have found a design that you like, draw very lightly around the "flowers." Or just make a dot in the center of each as a guide. Draw the stems and mark the place where the leaves will be.

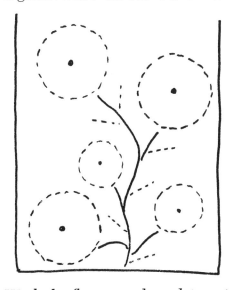

Work the flowers in *lazy daisy stitches* or in *long-tailed daisies*.
Work the stems in *outline stitches*.
Add leaves in *lazy daisy stitches*.

Cut out your finished work. Spread a thin coat of white glue on the notebook cover. Wait a few minutes until the glue becomes sticky; then press on your embroidered work and allow it to dry completely.

Straight Stitches

The *straight stitch* is the simplest stitch there is, and you now know enough to use it well. The needle comes up and goes down again, in any direction you choose, to make a stitch any length you want. It can be worked in groups to make flowers and leaves or scattered around to make grass or rain or fur or anything you can imagine. It is also a starting point for many other stitches.

To make flowers,
decide where you want to make
the center and come up
from the wrong side.
Work *straight stitches*
from the center toward the outside,
like spokes in a wheel.
Always come up near the same spot
in the center.
You can make as many "petals"
as you want, all the same
length or in different lengths.

You can also leave the center
open and work another
smaller flower with a closed center
on top of the first one.

You can create another
kind of flower
by working *straight stitches*
that go from one side of the circle
to the other and cross
at the center.
Use as many stitches as you want,
but try to make them all
cross at the same spot.

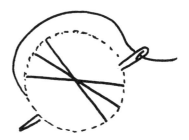

If the flower you are making
is a big one,
come up through the center
and make one or two small stitches
over the threads where they cross
at the center to hold down
the long stitches.

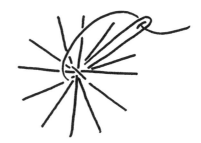

To make leaves,
come up at the end of the leaf
and work a center line
of *running stitches*.

Then work a row of *straight stitches*
at an angle to the *running stitches*.
Make them close together
or far apart, even or uneven.
But try to keep the angle the same.
Do the same thing on the
opposite side of the line.

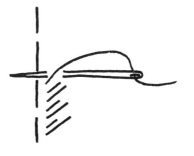

To make grass that grows
helter-skelter in meadows,
make helter-skelter stitches.

For grass that grows
in tidy clumps,
or for short stems of little
flowers, make three stitches
of different lengths.
Come up with the needle
at the same place
for all three of them.

Embroidering a Pillowcase

After you have found out some of the things you can do with *straight stitches*, use them to embroider the border of a pillowcase.

Use a plain white or colored pillowcase and embroidery floss in any colors you like. Remember that leaves don't have to be green, and flowers can be any colors that please you.

Decide what kind of design you want to make. You can scatter a field of flowers and grass along the border, on both sides or on just one side of the case.

Or you can lay out an even pattern.

Or you can arrange a single bunch of flowers and leaves.
Whichever way you choose, try to keep your design simple.
Use coins or buttons and strips of paper to work out the design.
Don't put the design too close to the edge of the hem, or it will
be hard to use the embroidery hoop. When you are satisfied with
the way it looks, draw lightly around each coin. Or put dots in
the centers, if you can do them freehand. Mark where the leaves
will begin and end.

Then begin working *straight stitches*. You will soon discover which
way of working is best for you—starting at the center or at the
left or right side, doing all the leaves first or all the flowers
first, or finishing each section as you go.

Don't worry if the stitches sometimes seem a bit lopsided and
uneven. You don't need to be perfect for this kind of stitching.
And you'll be so pleased with what you've done that you might even
want to embroider a sheet to match.

Satin Stitches

The *satin stitch* is made by working *straight stitches* so close together that they touch. It is a bit harder than the *straight stitch* because it must be done very evenly to look nice. But the finished embroidery is so lovely that it is worth working at.

Practice the *satin stitch*
by filling in a square.
Draw a ½-inch square
on your cloth.
Come up at one corner
and make a *straight stitch*
right across the square.
Come up again right next to
the beginning of the first stitch.
Make a second stitch beside it.
Keep the stitches straight
and even and close together.

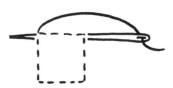
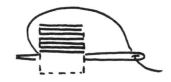

When you have filled a square,
try filling a circle.
Keep the circle small.
Use a button or coin
to draw a pattern.

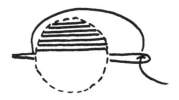

To make the *padded satin stitch*
that is used for flower centers,
work the usual *satin stitches*.
Then turn your work and
and do another set of *satin stitches*
across the first ones
in the other direction.

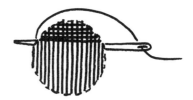

44

If you are having trouble keeping the edges neat, first go around the shape with *back stitches* (if you are using embroidery floss) or with *split stitches* (if you are using yarn). Then make the *satin stitches* right over them.

Or if you decide when you have finished that the edges are not as smooth and even as you would like them to be, try going around the edges with *back stitches* or *split stitches* to cover the uneven ends of the *satin stitches.*

Making a Card Case

One of the nicest ways to use the *satin stitch* is for a monogram— either your own initials or the initials of someone for whom you are making a special gift, arranged to form a design. They can be simple or very fancy with swirly letters. Sometimes they are so swirly you can't read them.

Small monograms decorate handkerchiefs and collars. Big bold ones appear on towels and bedspreads. You can start by monogramming a case for holding credit cards or embroidery needles, using plain, unswirly capital letters.

You will need a piece of cloth 11 inches long and 5 inches wide. Measure and mark the cloth, but don't cut it out. Instead, cut a piece of paper the same size. Measure and mark half an inch from each side along the long edges of the paper to show you where the seams will be.

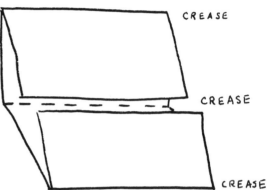

Fold the paper in half across the middle. Then fold both ends in to meet at the center crease and form two pockets.

You can put a monogram on only one pocket or on both. You can use two initials for the monogram or three. Sometimes the initial of the last name is made larger or put in the center of the monogram. If you were working a monogram for Martha Custis Washington, for instance, it could be mcw or ^McW or mWc or just mw.

If you want to monogram both pockets, remember to face the designs in opposite directions.

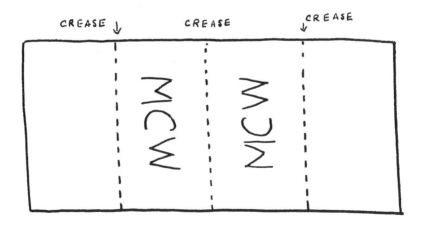

After you have worked out the design on the paper, unfold the paper
and copy the monogram onto the cloth.

Then begin working the stitches.
First work a row of *chain stitches*
over each letter.
For large letters work
another row of *chain stitches*
next to the first one.

Then work short *satin stitches*
right across the *chain stitches*.
Curves and corners are harder
to do than straight lines,
but you will soon learn how
to crowd your stitches when necessary
and to sew on top of others
when you have to.

After you have embroidered the monogram, cut out the piece of
cloth. Measure half an inch along each of the short ends to
make a little hem and fold it toward the wrong side. Pin and baste
the hems and sew them with little *hemming stitches*.

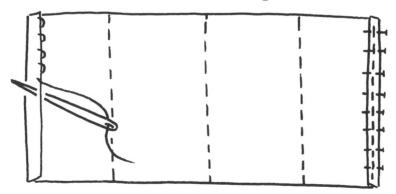

Then fold the cloth in half with the right side on the inside. Crease it with your fingers. Open it again and fold the ends in toward the crease to form two pockets. But leave half an inch between each hem and the center crease. Pin the sides and baste them.

Measure and mark half an inch from the side edges. Sew the seams with small *running stitches,* taking a *back stitch* every now and then to make the seams stronger.

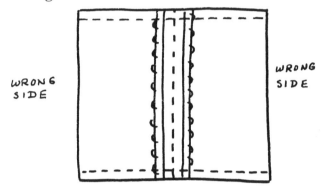

Trim about one-quarter of an inch from both seams with scissors. Turn the pockets right side out. Tack down the part of the seam that shows between the pockets with tiny *hemming stitches.*

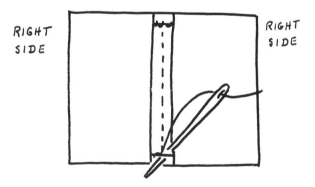

Blanket Stitches

The *blanket stitch* begins with a loop, and so it is a cousin of the *chain stitch* and the *lazy daisy*. Like the other stitches that you have learned, you can make the *blanket stitch* look different just by changing the size of the stitches and by working them close together or far apart.

When you are first learning how, it is easier to make neat *blanket stitches* on checked cloth with ¼-inch squares.

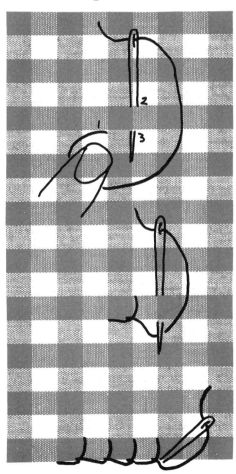

Work from left → to right.
Come up from the wrong side
at corner #1.
Hold the thread against the cloth
with your left thumb.
Go down at corner #2,
but don't let go of the thread.
Come up again at corner #3.

Pull the thread through
the loop that forms.
Don't pull it too tight.
Hold the thread again
and go down at corner #2
of the next square to the right.

When you come to the end
of the row,
go down again at corner #3
to hold the last stitch in place.

When you can do the *blanket stitch* on checked cloth, try it on plain cloth. Draw a bottom line as a guide.

Then try making stitches
of different lengths,
with the spaces between them even.

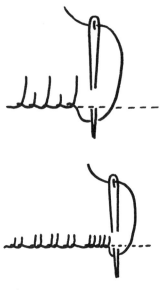

Then try making the spaces
between the stitches
of different widths.
If you work the stitches
so close together that they touch
or almost touch,
you are making the *buttonhole stitch*.
It is used for making buttonholes,
of course, and for embroidery
designs, too.

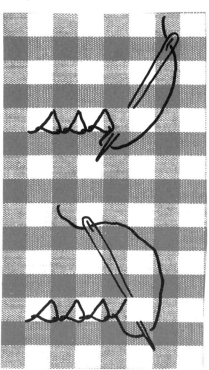

You can make a pretty stitch
called the *closed blanket stitch*
by making pairs of stitches.
Go down at corner #2
for the first stitch of the pair,
but instead of coming up
exactly at corner #3,
come up half a square to the left of it.

Go down at the *same* corner #2
for the second stitch of the pair,
and come up half a square
to the *right* of corner #3.

Then try working the *blanket stitch* along the edge of the cloth.
First, make a hem. Fold one-quarter of an inch of the cloth toward
the wrong side. Crease it with your fingers or a warm iron.
Then fold it over again to make a double hem. Pin it and baste it.

Hold the cloth with the edge down
and the right side toward you.
Hide the knot in the fold of the hem
and bring the needle out
along the crease.
Use the width of the hem
as a guide for making the stitch.

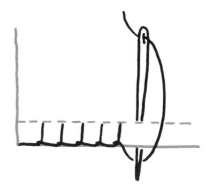

Practice going around corners, too. But first, turn, pin, and
baste a hem along the second edge, just as you did the first edge.

The easiest way to turn the corner
is to go through the very tip
of the corner and begin the second edge.

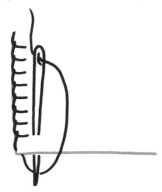

But there is a better way
that makes strong, neat corners
when you have practiced
and can do it well.
Turn the corner by making
four or five stitches close together,
instead of just one.

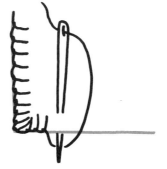

Making a Doll's Blanket

The *blanket stitch* is used for finishing edges and for working designs. If you make a blanket for your doll, you will find several ways of using different kinds of *blanket stitches.*

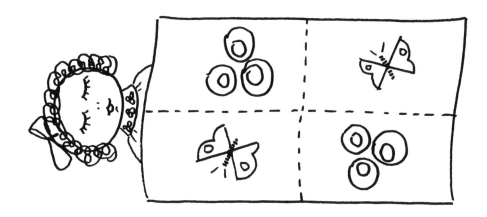

Decide how big you want the blanket to be and what kind of cloth you want to use. A plain pillowcase, if it is the right size for your doll, is easy to work with. It will also save you many stitches later because you will not have to sew the seams on three sides.

If you don't use a pillowcase, you will need two pieces of cloth that are the same size. One is for the front, where you will embroider your design. The second piece is left plain for the back, to cover the wrong side of your stitches. They can be the same color or two different colors that look nice together.

Cut each piece an inch wider and an inch longer than you want the finished blanket to be. Measure and mark half an inch from the edges for seams. Cut off the hem of the pillowcase, if you are using one, and measure and mark half an inch from the cut edge only.

Then work out your design.
You don't need to be an artist
to make up a design.
You can make some beautiful patterns
with just a few straight lines and circles.
For instance, a butterfly emerges from
a big "X" with buttons or coins as patterns
for the spots on the wings.

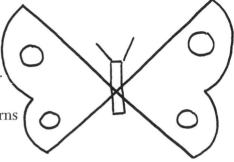

And you can draw around a cup
or a spool of thread or a thimble
to make flowers like zinnias.
Make them any size you want.

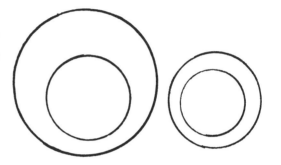

Cut out circles and butterfly shapes in different sizes from paper
and arrange them on the cloth until you have a design that you
like. Then pin the paper patterns on the cloth and draw around
them lightly.

You can make one large overall design
or you can divide the blanket in quarters
and work a small design in each section.

You can make the sections all alike
or in pairs or each one different.
But try to keep it simple
so that you don't get tired of working
on it before you are finished.

Choose thread or yarn in your favorite colors. But instead of using many different colors, try using the same three colors in different ways for all of the flowers. Then add a fourth color to the other three for the butterflies.

If you are making a blanket in four sections,
begin by sewing a *running stitch* down the center
and then across the middle
to divide it first in half and then in quarters.
Use one of your main colors for the *running stitch*.
(If you are using a pillowcase, be careful to make
these and all the other stitches only on one side
and not through both sides of the case.)
Go around the butterfly wings with *blanket stitch*.
Work the body of the butterfly in *satin stitch*
over two rows of *chain stitch*.
Fill the wing spots with *satin stitch*
or go around them with *buttonhole stitch*.
Do the antennae in *back stitch*.

Go around the outside circles of the flowers
with different kinds of *blanket stitches*.
Work the centers of the flowers in *padded satin stitch*.

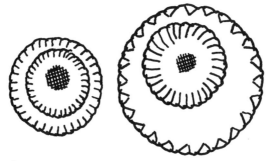

If you are making stems and leaves, work them in some
of the other stitches that you know, or try using
satin stitch and *blanket stitch* for them, too.

When you have finished the embroidery, put the back and front pieces together with the right sides on the inside. (If you used a pillowcase to make the blanket, you will not need to do this. Skip down to the line, "Turn your work right side out.")

Pin the pieces together around three sides. Leave one of the short sides unpinned. Baste the other three sides. Measure half an inch from each edge and mark the cloth to show you where to sew. Begin in the one corner and sew around three sides with *running stitches.*

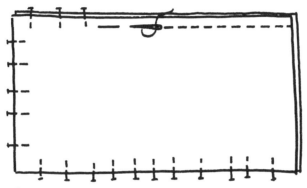

Turn your work right side out.

Now turn to the inside the edges that are not sewed. Pin them and baste them with large *running stitches.* You can sew the edges together with *overcast stitches* so small that they scarcely show.

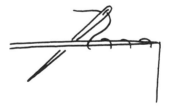

Or you can finish all the edges with a *blanket stitch* in one of your main colors. This is a big job that will take time.

If you like the blanket, maybe you will want to make a little doll's pillow to go with it.

CHAPTER 4

Appliqué and Still More Stitches

Appliqué (pronounced *ap-lee-KAY*) is a French word that means "put on" or "lay on." It is a way of laying one kind of cloth on top of another and sewing it in place to form a design. Sometimes it is decorated with embroidery stitches. Many old-fashioned quilts were made by *appliqué*. And when Betsy Ross sewed the thirteen white stars on the dark blue field for the first American flag, she was doing a patriotic *appliqué*.

Making an Appliqué Flag

You can begin by making a miniature version of Betsy Ross's American flag to hang in your room. Or you can make a flag with all the stars. After that you might want to design and make a special flag for your club.

Although you can make a flag of any size, this one is planned to be 6½ inches long and 10 inches wide. You will need plain cloth in red, white, and blue. Cut a piece of white cloth 7½ inches long and 11 inches wide for the background. Measure and mark half an inch from each edge for a hem.

Cut seven strips of red cloth 11 inches long and 1 inch wide. Fold the edges of each strip toward the center so they meet. Press them and baste the edges.

Lay the red stripes on the white background with a ½-inch stripe of white showing between each red one. Begin and end with half an inch of white at the top and bottom for hems.

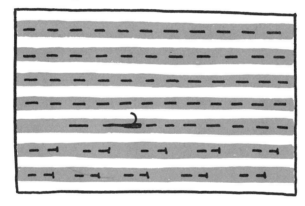

Pin the stripes and baste them down the center with large *running stitches*. Then sew each red stripe along both edges with little *hemming stitches*. This is the stitch most often used for *appliqué*.

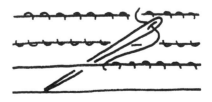

Next, cut a piece of blue cloth 4½ inches long and 5½ inches wide. Measure and mark half an inch from each side. Turn the edges under and baste them with large *running stitches.*

Pin the blue patch in the upper-left corner of the flag, half an inch from the top and half an inch from the left side of the flag. Baste the blue patch with *running stitches.* Sew all around it with *hemming stitches.*

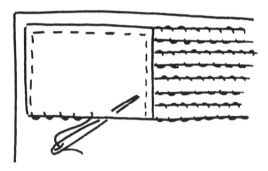

Star Stitch

If you are going to make a flag like Betsy Ross's, draw a circle in the middle of the blue field with chalk. Then mark places around the circle for thirteen stars. Try to space them evenly.

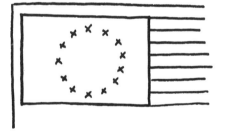

Use three strands of white embroidery floss to make the stars. Come up from the wrong side and make one small *cross stitch.* Then make another *cross stitch* over it, between the arms of the first cross. Finish with a third tiny *cross stitch* in the center to hold down the threads.

There are two ways to finish the flag.

You can sew a lining to the back. Cut a piece of plain cloth 7½ inches long and 11 inches wide. Put the flag and the lining together with the right sides on the inside. Pin and baste around three sides. Measure and mark half an inch from each edge. Leave open the short end where the stars are. Sew with little *running stitches*.

Turn the flag right side out. Turn in the edges that have not been sewed. Pin and baste them and sew them with *overcast stitches*.

Or you can fold under the hems on all four sides of the flag. Then turn under a little bit of the cut edge. Pin the hems, baste them, and sew them with tiny *hemming stitches*. Be careful not to let your stitches show on the right side.

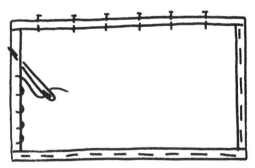

Staple the flag to a stick or wooden dowel. Or sew it to the stick with big *overcast stitches* that go right around the stick. Tie yarn or string to the ends of the stick for hanging.

Catch Stitch

The *catch stitch* is both useful and pretty.
It is a good way to join together the edges of two pieces of cloth.
And its zigzag design is a favorite embroidery stitch.
It is a fine stitch for *appliqué* because it does two things
at the same time: it joins the pieces of cloth and it decorates them.
The *catch stitch* can be worked in different ways.
Sometimes you might hear it called a *herringbone stitch*.

When you are first learning how, it is easier to make neat
catch stitches on checked cloth with ¼-inch squares.
Work from left → to right.
Come up from the wrong side
at corner #1.
Go down at corner #2,
and come up again a little way
to the left of it. Go down at corner #3
and come up a little way to the left of it.

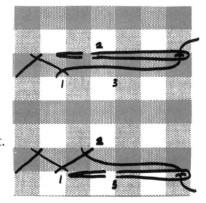

When you can do the *catch stitch* on checked cloth, try it on plain
cloth. Draw two lines one-quarter of an inch apart as a guide.
Then try it without any lines.

Try working stitches close together and do some that are long and *still* close together. That means they will be more straight up-and-down instead of at an angle.

And try working a second row of *catch stitches* between the first ones in a different color thread.

Making a Pajama Pillow

Here is a pillow to decorate your bed and to hide your pajamas or nightgown in during the day. You make it by *appliquéing* rectangles and triangles on a piece of background cloth. Then add embroidery stitches, such as the *catch stitch*.

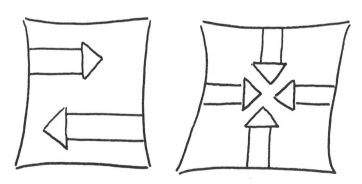

A pillow 12 inches long and 12 inches wide is just large enough to hide a pair of pajamas. Choose the cloth you want to use for the background. Cut one piece 13 inches wide and 13 inches long. Measure and mark half an inch all around for seams.

Then cut out some paper rectangles and triangles in different sizes and arrange them on the cloth to make a design. For example, you can make a pattern of arrows by putting a triangle at the end of a long, narrow rectangle.

Make all the arrows the same size, or make them different sizes. Point them in the same direction or in different directions, or even overlap them.

When you have the design you want, pin the paper shapes to the cloth. Draw lightly around each shape to show you where each piece will go.

Then make a *template* for each size of rectangle and triangle that you plan to use. To make a template, lay the paper pattern on a piece of cardboard. Draw around it and cut it out. Keep the edges of the cardboard smooth.

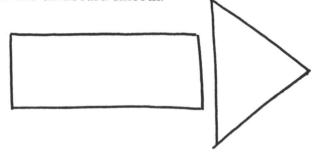

Search through your box of scraps to find pieces of cloth for the arrows. You can use plain or printed cloth. You can cut all the arrows from the same cloth or use several different kinds. The important thing is to have the different kinds of cloth go well together.

When you have decided all these things, lay the template on the cloth and draw around it. Then with a ruler add an extra quarter of an inch all around for hems.

Cut out each piece
along the outside line.
Lay the template on the wrong side
of the piece. Turn up the ¼-inch hem
along each side of the template.
Use a warm iron to press the hems
with the template still in place.
Corners are tricky. Do your best
to keep them neat.
Take away the template and baste
the hems with *running stitches*.
Make sure the corners are held
down tightly.

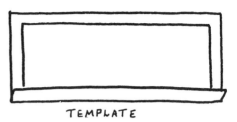

TEMPLATE

Lay the finished *appliqué* pieces right side up on the background cloth. Pin them in place and baste them with *running stitches*. Then go around each shape with *catch stitches*.

Make the stitches small and
close together so they will
hold down the *appliqué* pieces.

Or make them farther apart
and work a second row
in between them.

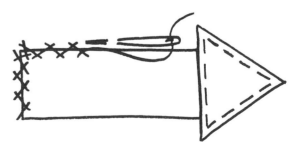

Add any other stitches you want. Work them right on top of the *appliquéd* pieces or in between them. But they should be part of the design and not just an added-on idea.

For the back of the 12-inch pillow, you will need two pieces of cloth, each 13 inches long and 9 inches wide. Measure and mark one inch on one long edge of each piece for hems. Fold each hem to the wrong side and press it with your fingers or with a warm iron. Turn under a little bit of the cut edge. Pin it and baste it. Sew it with *hemming stitches*. Make the stitches so that they hardly show on the right side.

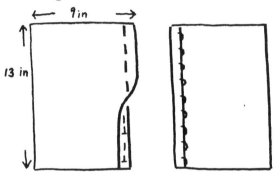

You are going to put the two pieces for the back together so that they overlap. This makes a hidden opening for taking your pajamas out of the pillow and putting them back.

Measure three inches from the hemmed edge of one piece and mark it. Lay the hemmed edge of the second piece along the marks. This makes them overlap. Pin the overlapping hems together at each end and baste them.

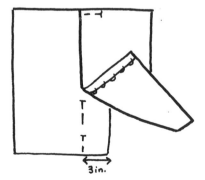

Put the right sides of the pillow together. Pin and baste them on all four sides. Measure and mark half an inch from each side for seams. Sew all around with the little *running stitches*. Turn the pillow right side out through the opening in the back. Use your pajamas for stuffing, or use anything else that you want to keep out of sight.

French Knots

Did you ever think a knot might be a stitch?
The French kind is.
One big *French knot* can make an animal's eye
with a single stitch.
Lots of them close together can make a lion's mane.

A sprinkle of French knots might be lots of little flowers growing in a field,
or the center of a single flower in a vase.

French knots need a little more practice than most other stitches to make them come out exactly the way you want them. Don't be discouraged if the first ones look straggly. Practice is the only cure for that. You can decide if the results are worth it.

You will need both hands for this,
so sit near a table where you can
lay the embroidery hoop down.

Come up from the wrong side
at the place where you want
to make a knot.

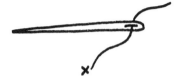

Hold the needle close to the cloth
with your right hand.
With your left hand, wrap the thread
around the needle three times.
Hold on to the thread
so that it doesn't unwind or slide off.

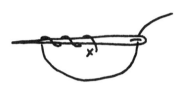

Then go down close to the spot
where you first came up.
Let go of the thread.
Pull the needle through slowly,
and the thread will curl
itself into a knot.

Making an Apron

You will need a piece of cloth 16 inches wide and 16 inches long.
It can be plain cloth or one with a very small pattern, like
stripes or dots or checks or tiny flowers. You will also need
a piece of ribbon 48 inches long and about 1 inch wide. If you
don't have ribbon, you can make one with strips of cloth.

Measure and mark two inches from the top and bottom for hems.
Measure and mark one inch from each side for hems.

Draw circles on paper, using lids or saucers or drinking glasses as patterns. Cut them out. The circles will become flowers. Lay the paper circles on the cloth to make a design of flowers. Put small circles inside large ones. Overlap some of the circles.

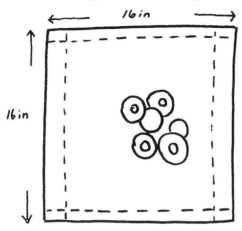

After you have arranged the flowers the way you want them, pin the circles to the cloth and draw lightly around each one to show you where the pieces will go.

Now make a cardboard *template* for each size circle. Search through your box of scraps to find pieces of cloth for the flowers. Plain cloth is best. You can make all the flowers from the same material or use as many different colors as you like. Just be sure they go together well and show up against the background.

Lay the cardboard template on the cloth and draw around it. Add on an extra quarter of an inch all around for hems. Unless you have a compass, draw the outside circle freehand.

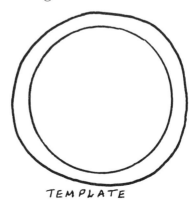

TEMPLATE

Cut out the circles.
Lay the template on the wrong side
of the circle. Turn up the ¼-inch hem
around the template and use
a warm iron to press the hem
with the template still in place.
Take away the template
and baste around the circle
with small *running stitches*
to hold down the fullness.

Lay the circles on the cloth. Pin them in place and baste them
with *running stitches.* Sew them with any of the stitches you
have learned. *Hemming stitches* go faster, but *catch stitches* and
blanket stitches look very nice, especially on plain cloth.

If you are putting smaller circles
inside the larger ones,
sew them on next.

Then with yarn or thread
in a color that shows up well
against the cloth, make some
French knots in the center
of each flower.
Make them very close together,
or sprinkle just a few.

Add any other stitches that you like for stems and leaves,
or let the flowers bloom just the way they are.

To finish the apron, first turn the side hems to the wrong side. Press the hems. Turn under a little bit of the cut edge. Pin and baste each edge and sew it with little *hemming stitches.* Sew the top and bottom hems the same way.

The top hem makes a casing or "tunnel" for the ribbon to go through. Fasten a safety pin to one end of the ribbon and use that to pull the ribbon through the casing.

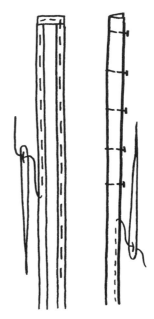

If you don't have ribbon, you can make a tie from a strip of cloth. Use cloth that matches the apron or one of the flowers. You will need a piece 3 inches wide and 48 inches long. You can cut two or three shorter pieces and sew the ends together to make one long strip.

Turn a little bit of all the cut edges toward the wrong side and press them with your fingers or a warm iron. Baste around all four edges. Fold the strip in half the long way with the wrong side on the inside. Pin the edges together evenly. Sew with *running stitches* close to one long edge and across the two ends. Fasten a safety pin to one end and use that to pull the strip through the casing. Tie the ribbon around your waist. Push the apron to the front so that it makes gathers.

Couching

Couching is also a way to lay something on top of
a background of cloth. The "something" is not another piece
of cloth, like *appliqué.* It is usually a piece of yarn or
ribbon or string that is too thick to be stitched *through*
the cloth, and so it is stitched *on* the cloth. The "something"
can also be a small object—a bit of metal, a smooth pebble,
a seashell, a feather, a piece of wood or bark or grass.

First try *couching* down a piece of yarn or string. Draw a line
on the cloth to show you where to put the yarn. Begin with a
straight line. Then try a curve and then a loop.

The thread in your needle can
be the same color as the yarn
you are *couching,* or it can be
another color.

Work from right ← to left.
Lay the yarn on the line
you have drawn.
Hold it there with your left thumb.
Come up from the wrong side.
Make a *straight stitch* across
the yarn, going down again
at almost the same spot.

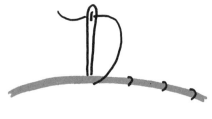

Come up again a short distance away
and make another stitch.
Try to space the *couching stitches*
evenly. You might need to make them
closer together on tight corners.

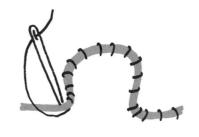

There are some other ways
to do *couching*.
You can make slanting stitches
like *hemming stitches*.

Or you could use *blanket stitches*
or *catch stitches* to hold down
the piece of yarn or string.

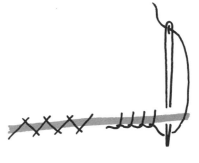

To *couch* a small object,
make a few *straight stitches*
back and forth across it.
Use enough stitches to
hold it in place.

Making a Zippered Bag

You can *couch* a design on a zippered bag for carrying pencils
and things. You will need a 7-inch zipper and two pieces of cloth,
each 8 inches long and 4 inches wide. Draw around the pieces,
but don't cut them out until you have finished stitching them.
Measure and mark half an inch from each side to show you where
the seams will be.

71

Couching is a good way to make interesting abstract designs that don't look like anything in particular. You can let your yarn make its own wandering pattern on the cloth and *couch* it down as you go.

Or you can draw a crisscross pattern of straight lines on the cloth and *couch* down different kinds of yarn and ribbon along the lines. Carry the ends of the yarn past the seam lines so that they will be finished neatly when you sew the seams.

 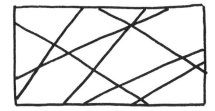

When you have finished the *couching,* cut out the pieces of cloth. Turn under the ½-inch hem on one long edge of each piece and baste it. Lay the zipper right side up on a table. Lay the pieces of cloth right side up so that the hems just touch the sides of the zipper teeth. Pin the pieces of cloth to the zipper and baste them. Sew close to the zipper with small *back stitches.*

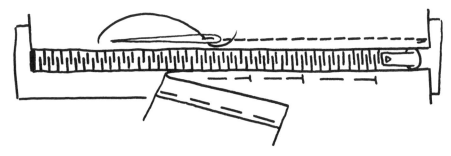

Open the zipper and bring the wrong sides of the two pieces of cloth together so that the edges are even. Pin around the three open sides and baste them. Sew them with *running stitches.* Turn the bag right side out through the open zipper.

CHAPTER 5

Needlepoint

Needlepoint is another ancient form of embroidery. It is usually done with thick yarn on special canvas. The stitches are simple. Some are like the embroidery stitches you already know. They completely cover the canvas. Needlepoint can be fine enough to decorate a tiny box, or big and heavy enough to make a rug. You can learn to do both.

Needlepoint canvas is woven with openings between the threads. Sometimes pairs of threads are woven together to make *double-thread canvas*. Sometimes the threads are evenly spaced to make *single-thread canvas*.

The places where the threads cross are called *meshes*.
If there are 14 meshes to an inch, the spaces between the threads are very small, and you use fine yarn and a small needle to make the tiny stitches.

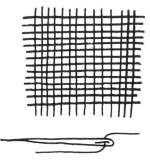

If there are only three or four meshes
to an inch, the spaces between
the threads are large, and you use
thick yarn and a big needle
to make big, bold stitches.
Rugs are made on canvas this size.
It is easier and faster
to work with canvas
with large spaces.

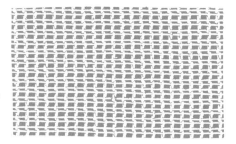

The kind most people
know about is double-thread
canvas with ten meshes to an inch.

For your beginning projects, it is not important what kind of canvas
you have. In fact, you don't even need to use needlepoint canvas.
You can use any cloth that has thick, even threads, like burlap
or monk's cloth. The color doesn't matter because the stitches
will cover it.

You use a tapestry needle, which has a blunt end and a large eye
that is easy to thread. Needlepoint canvas is very stiff,
so you do not need to use an embroidery hoop.

Use whatever yarn you have. If you are using small mesh canvas,
you will need fine yarn. If the mesh is large, you can use heavy
rug yarn or two or three pieces of ordinary yarn together.
Cut the yarn in pieces about 20 inches long. Don't put a knot in
the end.

Half-Cross Stitches

The *half-cross stitch* makes a slanting stitch on the right side
of the canvas and a straight stitch on the wrong side.
Work from left → to right.
Come through from the wrong side.
Leave a one-inch "tail" of yarn
on the wrong side.
Count up one space
and one space to the right,
and go through with the needle.
Count down one space
and come back through from
the wrong side.

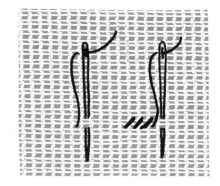

Always go straight through the canvas and make each stitch
in two parts. Don't try to do the parts together, as you
would if you were sewing a *running stitch.*

Once in a while, if the yarn seems to be getting kinky,
let the needle hang down loose and unwind itself.

When you come to the end of the row, turn your work
completely around so that the top is at the bottom.
Begin the next row above it. Each stitch will share a space
with the stitch below it, so that all of the background threads
are covered. As you reach the end of the second row, try to
catch the "tail" of yarn that you left on the wrong side
and fasten it down in the next few stitches. That will keep it
from coming loose. At the end of each row, turn your work
completely around again.

When you want to end or change to another color, fasten off the yarn. Weave the needle in and out of the stitches on the wrong side of your work.

You can make a longer stitch by counting up two spaces or even three spaces. But you can count only one space to the right.

Decorating a Box

If you have a small, strong cardboard box, you can decorate the top with a piece of needlepoint. Lay the lid on the canvas (or whatever cloth you are using) and draw around it with pen, marker, or even crayon because the marks will be covered up by the yarn. Then with a ruler add half an inch all around for turning under.

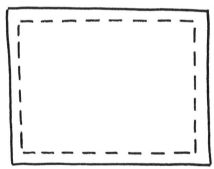

Try to have yarn in two or three different colors. (This is a good way to use up odds and ends of yarn.) Now plan a design made of rows of *half-cross stitches* in different sizes and colors.

Work some rows of stitches one space high. Make some rows two spaces and some three spaces high. Use a different color for each size stitch. You could end up with something like this:

blue—three rows of three spaces high
yellow—two rows of two spaces high
green—six rows of one space high
yellow—two rows of two spaces high
blue—three rows of three spaces high

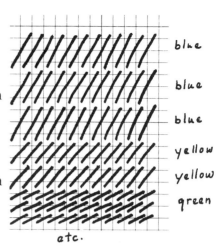

blue
blue
blue
yellow
yellow
green
etc.

Begin and end the rows of stitches at the line you drew around the lid. The half an inch for turning under will not have any stitching.

When you have finished the needlepointing, turn the half an inch to the wrong side. Sew it to the back of the stitches with large *hemming stitches.*

Spread white glue on the top of the lid. Put the piece of needlepoint on top of it. Let it dry. Decorate the sides of the lid and the box with colored paper.

Gros Point and Petit Point

Gros point (pronounced *GROW point*) and *petit point* (*PETTY point*) are the French names for two slanting stitches.
Petit point means "little stitch."
It is made over just one mesh,
usually on very small-mesh canvas.
Gros point means "large stitch."
It is the same stitch made larger.

77

Work from right ← to left.
Come through from the wrong side,
leaving a one-inch "tail."
For *petit point,* count up one space
and one space to the right,
and go through with the needle.
(This first step was like the
half-cross stitch. It is the
second step that makes it different.)
Count down one space
and two spaces to the *left.*
so that you come through to the *left*
of the stitch you have just made.

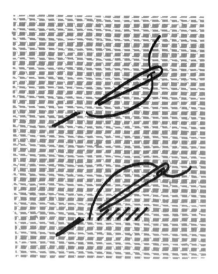

When you come to the end of the row, turn your work completely
around so that the top is at the bottom. Begin the next row above it.

Here are three ways to do *gros point:*
Count up two spaces
and two spaces to the right.

Or count up two spaces
and one space to the right.

Or count up one space
and two spaces to the right.

Go through with the needle
to the wrong side.
Come back through to the *left*
of the stitch you have just made.

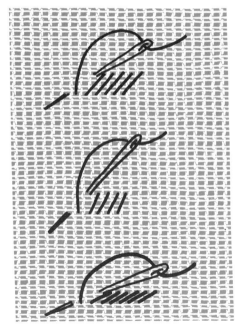

Making a Hot Mat or Dollhouse Rug

You can use *petit point* and *gros point* to make a handsome mat to put
under hot dishes on the table or to use as a rug in a doll's house.
If you work the design in two-inch squares, you can arrange the
squares to make the mat or rug the shape and size you want.

Decide how many squares long and how many squares wide you want
the mat to be. Draw the squares on the canvas. With a ruler add
half an inch all around for a hem. Draw a one-inch square inside
each two-inch square.

Then plan the colors. You can use two colors of yarn and work all
the small inside squares in one color and all the large outside
squares in a second color. Of course, you can also make the squares
in as many colors as you like.

First, work the small inside
squares in *petit point*.

Then, work the large outside
squares in *gros point*.

When you have finished the needlepointing, turn the ½-inch hem to
the wrong side. Sew it to the back of the needlepoint stitches with
large *hemming stitches*.

You should make a backing for your mat or rug. If you have some felt, you can cut a piece the same size as the needlepoint and glue it to the back.

Or you can cut a piece of cloth one inch wider and one inch longer than the needlepoint. Turn under half an inch on each edge of the cloth. Pin it and baste it. Sew it to the back with *overcast stitches.*

Satin Stitches Again

Satin stitches are easier to make on canvas than on cloth because the heavy canvas threads keep your stitches straight and even. Before you begin the up-and-down stitches, draw a line across the canvas. That will be the top guideline. Then count down eight spaces and draw the bottom guideline. (You can also work this stitch on burlap or other coarse cloth.)

Work from left → to right.
Come through from the wrong side
on the top guideline.
Count down three or four spaces and
go back through to the wrong side.
Count one space to the right
and come through again
on the top line.

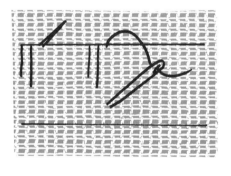

Make the next stitch either longer
or shorter than the one before it.
Make some almost down to the
bottom line. Make some very short.

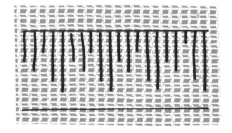

When you have worked a row of long and short *satin stitches*, fasten off your yarn. Then put another color yarn in the needle.

Now come up from the wrong side
on the bottom line.
Make the stitch long enough
to meet the one above it.
The length of each stitch
on the top row will show
you how long to make
each stitch on the bottom row.

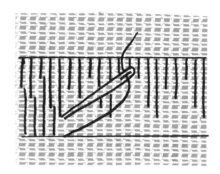

After you have worked these two rows of stitches that are different lengths, try making an even pattern of long-and-short stitches. Draw a top guideline. Count down eight spaces and draw the bottom guideline.

Work from left → to right.
Come through from the wrong side
on the top guideline.
Count down two spaces and go back through.
Come through again on the top line.

Make each stitch one space longer
than the one before it
until the stitch covers six spaces.
Then make each stitch one space
shorter than the one before it
until you are back to *two* again.
Then begin making each stitch
longer again.

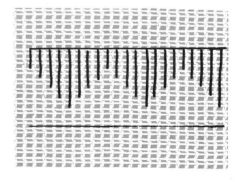

When you have worked an even pattern of long-and-short *satin stitches*,
fasten off your yarn. Put another color yarn in the needle.

Come through from the wrong side
on the bottom line.
Go up to meet the stitch above it.
You can cover a whole piece of canvas
with these long-and-short *satin stitches*.

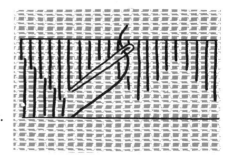

Making a Pincushion

Hundreds of years ago ladies liked to have fancy pincushions
to carry with them. They often decorated them with needlepoint,
and they called them "pyn pyllows" because of their shape.

Draw the size you want to make on the canvas. Make it twice as long
as it is wide. If it is three inches wide, it should be six inches long.
Add about one inch all around. This will give you enough space
to make the pattern come out even. And there will be enough
left over for seams.

Use yarn in two colors or more to work the pattern of long-and-short
satin stitches. Remember to catch in the "tails" of yarn and to
fasten off your yarn on the wrong side by winding in and out of
a few stitches.

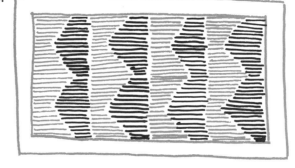

When you have finished the needlepoint, fold your work in half with the right side on the inside. Sew the two side seams together with tiny *running stitches.* Sew through the canvas as close to the needlepoint stitches as you can. Turn your work right side out. Stuff it with cotton or bits of cloth or an old stocking. Tuck in the edges of the canvas and sew the opening with *overcast stitches.* The "pyn pyllow" will be a treasure for any lady who likes to stitch.

Sawtooth Design

The *sawtooth design* is also made with *satin stitches.* The stitches are all the same size, but they are worked in up-and-down steps. The design is easy to do, but when you have finished, it looks as though it must have been very hard.

Work from left → to right.
Come through from the wrong side.
Count up two spaces and
go back through to make
one stitch.
Count down one space
and one space to the right,
and come through again.
Each stitch is two spaces long,
and each stitch is made one space
higher on the canvas
than the one before it.

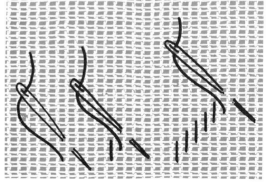

After you have made eight
or ten steps going *up*,
begin making steps going *down*.
Count down *three* spaces
and one space to the right,
and come through from the wrong side.
Count up two spaces and
go back through again.
Make steps going down
until you are even with
the first stitch in the pattern.

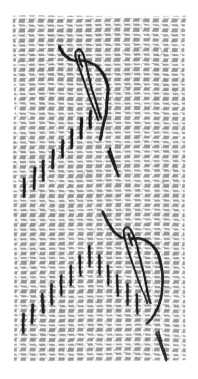

Do the up-and-down *sawtooth design* as many times as you want across
the canvas. Fasten off the yarn. Begin the second row right under
the first one. Use a different color yarn for the row. This is a
good pattern for using as many different colors as you like.

When you want to end the design,
fill in the "teeth" with shorter
and shorter rows of up-and-down
stitches. When there are only
small triangles left,
finish them with one color.

Making a Purse

You can use the *sawtooth design* to make a purse for yourself or a handbag for your doll.

Mark a piece of canvas 4 inches wide and 8 inches long. Add half an inch all around for seams and cut it out. Draw a line down the center of the canvas. Measure one inch on each side of the center line and draw two more lines. These lines will help to make the design work out evenly.

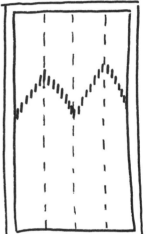

Begin your stitches about
halfway down the canvas.
Make step-up stitches
as far as the first line.
Then do step-down stitches
to the center line.
Step up to the third line.
Step down to the end.

Cover the canvas with the *sawtooth design* above and below that first row of stitches. Fill in the triangles at the top and bottom.

Turn the hems at the top and bottom to the wrong side.
Sew them with *hemming stitches*.

Sew a button 2½ inches from the bottom on the right side.

2½ in

Turn up the bottom three inches of the needlework so that the right side is on the inside. Sew the two side seams together with tiny *running stitches*. Sew through the canvas as close to the needlepoint stitches as you can. Turn the purse right side out. There will be a two-inch flap left at the top for closing the purse.

Turn down the hems along each side of the flap and sew them with *hemming stitches*.

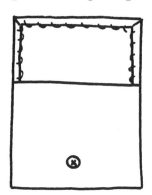

Cut three pieces of yarn, each about eight inches long. Knot them together at one end. Braid them to make a piece three inches long. Make a knot at the end of the braid. Trim off the extra yarn. Make a loop big enough to go over the button. Sew the ends of the loop on the wrong side of the flap near the edge.

You can make this coin purse into a handbag for a doll by adding a handle. Make the handle by braiding yarn as you did for the loop. Sew it to the top of each side seam.

CHAPTER 6

A Sampler for Christmas

A sampler is a picture made with all the stitches you have learned. You can use embroidery stitches with *appliqué* and needlepoint to make a sampler that is brought out every year at Christmastime. A needlework Christmas tree would make a very special gift for your family.

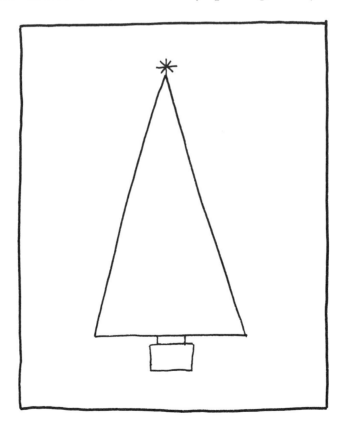

Because you will keep this sampler for many years, use good cloth for it. Use any colors you want. You could put a green tree on a bright red background and trim the tree with white stitches, or put a white tree on a dark background with stitches in many colors. Decide where the sampler will be hung and cut the background cloth to fit that space. Add half an inch all around for seams.

Cut a tall triangle from paper as a pattern for the tree. When you have found the right size and shape, use the paper pattern as a guide for cutting a template from cardboard. Lay the template on the cloth you are using for the tree and draw around it. Add an extra quarter of an inch on each side for hems. Cut out the triangle on the outside line.

Lay the template on the wrong side of the cloth. Turn up the hems along the sides of the template and press them with a warm iron. Take away the template and baste the hems with *running stitches.* Make sure the three corners are held down.

Pin the tree to the background cloth. Baste it with *running stitches.* Sew around it with little *hemming stitches.*

Now decorate the tree with stitches. Make single rows or work two or three rows close together to form a band of stitches.

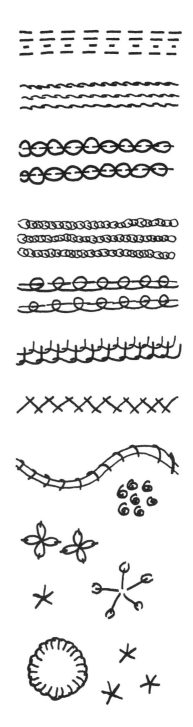

Between the bands, *couch* down loops of yarn or Christmas wrapping cord.

And between the bands and the loops, hang "ornaments" made from *French knots, daisies, buttonhole stitches,* and *straight stitches.*

Hang a *star stitch* on the very top.

Work the trunk of the tree
in *satin stitch*.

Plant the tree in a needlepoint tub.
Draw a square on the canvas. Add half
an inch all around. Work some of the
needlepoint stitches you know. Turn
under the half an inch and *appliqué*
the square to the background cloth.

Remember to put your name or initials
and your age and the date
in one corner of the sampler.

Make a lining for the sampler. Cut a piece of cloth the same size as the sampler. Pin them together with the right sides on the inside. Baste around the two sides and the bottom. Leave the top open. Measure and mark one inch from the top on each side seam. Sew the seams with little *running stitches,* beginning and ending at the marks. Turn the sampler right side out.

Measure and mark half an inch from the top.
Turn in the edges along the marks.
Pin and baste the edges. Sew with
overcast stitches.
There should be a ½-inch opening
at the top of each side seam.

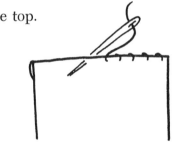

Find a dowel or smooth stick at least an inch wider than the sampler, or ask someone to cut a piece of a wire clothes hanger. Slide it in the top through the openings on each side seam. Tie a piece of yarn or ribbon on the ends of the stick to hang your new family treasure.

Index